Dream Big
And Live
Those Dreams

No Limitations Allowed

OLU OLABODE

Published by
HeartBeat Productions Inc.
Box 633
Abbotsford, BC Canada V2T 6Z8
email: info@heartbeat1.com
604 852.3769

ISBN: 978-1-895112-59-7

Edited by: Dr. Win Wachsmann
Cover design: Dr. Carrie Wachsmann

"If you can dream it, God can do it."

Terri Savelle Foy

"You are never too old to set another goal
or to dream a new dream."

C. S. Lewis

TABLE OF CONTENTS

A man's gift makes room for him, and brings him before great men.

Proverbs 18:16

ACKNOWLEDGMENTS

I would like to first thank the Almighty God for being such an awesome father to me. He alone blessed me with this gift of writing.

I would then like to thank my husband, David and my children, Fikayomi, Feranmi, Fiyibomi and Divine. There is no way I would have been able write this book without your support.

My next set of thanks goes to my number 1 mentor. Terri Savelle Foy. I have listened to you for over five years and you have been such a blessing to me, but most especially you have challenged me to do more and become more.

I would like to also thank members of RCCG Jesus House Abbotsford for your constant encouragement over the years.

I would like to say a special thank you to Tamara Unrau for proofreading this book and being so patient with me in the process of doing so. God bless you.

I would also like to say thank you to Matthew Unrau and Rali Macaulay for your endorsements of the book.

A special thank you also goes to my Editors and Publishers, Drs. Win and Carrie Wachsmann.

INTRODUCTION

Why another book on dreaming big dreams, you may wonder? It may be because the dreams in our heart are key to what God has wired us for on this earth.

A lot of times, most people do not function in what they have been called to do until an external force causes them to do so.

I would like you to see this book as a wake-up call that is set to rouse you out of "sleep." "Sleep" of just living day to day, "sleep" of living in the busyness of life and just passing through life. "Sleep of living within the confines of the box. Do you know what the "box" represents? It represents our comfort zone. It represents whatever does not inconvenience us. It represents "the normal day-to-day life. It represents the "9-5 job life" and whatever else the box might represent

When God created you and me, He created us for specific purposes. Everybody has a purpose. Each person in life has an assignment on his/her life and the dreams God puts in each person's heart is there to lead one towards that person's assignment or purpose. When you ignore such dreams, you lose track of how to fulfill your assignment.

Jesus had an assignment and He fulfilled it as can be seen in John 17:4a

"I glorified you on earth by completing down to the last detail what you assigned me to do."
John 17:4a The Message Bible

Will you be able to say the same at the end of your life? Are you even walking in the right direction? The gifts, talents, dreams God has blessed you with have only one purpose. It is to fulfill your "life" assignment and do all that God has called you to do and be during your time here.

As you read this book, I will like to encourage you to not only be informed but also to be stirred up to become all that God has created you to be.

I pray that you will choose to break out of the molds of life and **rise above everything that represents an obstacle in your life.**

It's time to dream big, believe those dreams and live them out. No limitations allowed!

CHAPTER 1

DREAMING STARTS THE PROCESS

What is a Dream?

You might wonder what a dream is. I am sure many people do. A dream connotes an iota of the imaginary; it indicates a picture of the unseen.

According to Noah Webster's 1828 Online Dictionary, a dream can refer to several things:

1. to have ideas or images in the mind
2. in the state of sleep

The kind of dreams I am referring to in this book are the ideas, images, and thoughts in your mind. The imaginations God brings into your mind as you desire to be all that He has created you to be.

A Scripture I've grown to love is *Ephesians 3:20*

20 Now to him who is able to do immeasurably more than all we ask or imagine, according to his power that is at work within us...

This passage reveals how it's up to me to dream and then up to God to do even much more than I can dream or imagine.

May I ask you a question?

How much would you be able to dream about if you had no barriers?

What are those yearnings in your heart that need to be expressed?

Dreaming is a process whereby you permit yourself to think freely.

Can anyone relate to what I am saying?

What are those dreams you have nursed in your heart since you were a child?

When I was a child, I used to write short stories, and I wrote a couple of them thinking that when the time was right, I was going to publish them. Guess what, I never did. I got carried away by the mundane things of life. I got caught up in the "busyness" of just going through the motions.

In your life, do you have any ideas or dreams that have been on your heart but seemed unachievable? They seemed bigger than what you could handle at the time. You will not be the first person to have those kinds of dreams and not the last.

You, however, are the only one who can choose to do "something" with those dreams.

What do I mean by "do something?" I mean it's time to act. It's time to get up and run with those dreams.

Let's look at the story of a man in the Bible called Abraham. He longed to have a son, he dreamed of having a son to take over all his possessions. He did not want a servant inheriting all that with which God had blessed him. He, however, thought it was impossible to have a child with his wife, Sarah. He did not see a way as he was close to one hundred years old and Sarah was also ninety years old. How would this happen? (*Genesis 21:1-3*)

This dream was bigger than Abraham, but guess what, he had a dream giver (God) and when the dream giver gives you a dream, He does not want you to fuss about the details of the dream. (How it's going to work and what you are going to need for it to work) No... God just wants you to run with the dream. He wants you to trust Him to help you bring the dream to pass.

Abraham tried to get into the details ("Oooh I'm too old, Sarah is past menopause. Is there anybody else that God can use other than Sarah?") As he got into the details, he began to come up with alternatives that were not in God's plan: Hagar and Ismael.

When you and I get into the details instead of asking Him to lead us, we get on the wrong path and it leads to mistakes (such as Abraham's) that can take years, decades or even centuries to correct.

Hagar and Ismael were not meant to be in his "dream journey," but he brought them in. Because of that, God went silent on him for a number of years. You can read the whole story in *Genesis 15:1-6, Genesis 16:1-15 and Genesis 17:1-27.*

God had put the dream in Abraham's heart by showing him the stars asking if he could count them, (*Genesis 15:5*) but God had not told Abraham how it was going to happen.

What are the dreams you have tried to work out yourself? What are the Ismael's that you try to birth by yourself instead of waiting on God to help you? Abraham did not know that the dream of having a son by Sarah was going to produce so many other "sons." He did not envision that he was going to become a father of nations.

How could a man who was 100 years old become a father of nations? How could he become a father to generations and generations after him? That could only start with a dream, and God used that dream to bring to pass his "life" assignment. (Being blessed and being a blessing to his world.)

Abraham had to go through all that he went through just to become a father to nations and a blessing to his world. That was what he was created for. We still speak of Abraham today because Abraham eventually yielded to God to help him bring that dream to pass in his life.

To encourage you, I will like to share my story.

When God rekindled my love for writing, I did not know how I was going to be able to bring anything to fruition. I just knew that I wanted to and loved to write. However, I did not know how I was going to publish my work. The only thing I did at the time was to listen and follow the instructions God gave me. As I followed those instructions, He began to open doors for me to walk through. Furthermore, as I followed those instructions, He brought people into my life to birth the dreams He has put in my heart.

Following instructions and being obedient is so important to God when He is leading you. He does not give us the full picture all at once. Like a puzzle, He gives you piece by piece until you have put all the pieces together and the puzzle is complete. Then you can see the full picture and understand your entire situation.

I would, however, encourage you not to rush to gather all the pieces before you start putting the puzzle together. Rather trust God to lead you in the right way.

Why is it so important to dream?

1. Dreaming enables you to see things from a fresh perspective. It creates an "I can do it mentality" in you.
2. In the place of dreaming, there are no fears; there are no barriers: there are just possibilities.

3. Dreaming challenges you. It enables you to stir yourself. It makes you believe you can achieve anything, if only you give yourself the task to perform.
4. Dreaming brings out the power in you. There is so much that God has placed on the inside of every man. He has given you the power to imagine and the power to accomplish.

CHAPTER 2

TOOLS FOR DREAMING

Tool 1: Your Vision:

What can you see? Vision is key.

In the dreaming process, Vision is key. The Cambridge dictionary defines vision as
- An idea or mental image of something.
- An experience in which you see things that do not exist physically when something powerfully affects your mind such as deep religious thoughts, drugs, or mental illness.

The Oxford dictionary(Oxforddictionary.com) defines it as:
- The faculty or state of being able to see.
- The ability to think about or plan the future with imagination or wisdom.

Vision is defined as the state of being able to see. It is the ability to think about or plan the future with imagination or wisdom.

Vision directs a human being's life in their day-to-day affairs. It is what you see that directs what you do. It is used to help you to function effectively.

Vision, however, goes beyond what you can see physically. A vision can also be defined as a mental image of something or an idea. It can be defined as "seeing with your mind." It is a process where you travel into your imagination and run with what you see.

If I ask you to think and visualize your life, what would you see?

How do envision your future?

What you see determines what you become. When what you see is constantly before you, it will inspire you to work towards it.

Let me ask you some questions that you can ponder.

Where will YOU be in 5 years?

What will YOU have accomplished in the next twelve months?

Remember Abraham? In *Genesis 13*, we learn that the land around Bethel was not big enough for both families. Abraham let Lot choose which land Lot wanted for his flocks.

After Lot chose, God spoke with Abraham and told him to look as far as he could he see. He promised to give Abraham and his generations as much land as he could **see. (*Genesis 13:14-17*)**

God knows the power of vision and emphasizes it in His word.

"Where there is no vision, the people perish but he that keepeth the law, happy is he"
Proverbs 29:18 KJV

What you see, you don't forget quickly.

What you see will often play over and over in your mind. It will often have a hold on you. When you act on what you see, it can take you further than you can imagine if you let it.

What you see can stir you up and wake up the potential in you if you let it.

What are those dreams, those visions, those goals that you've had in times past? Think back and see what you did with them. I would love to challenge you to pick them up right now, '**see**" and begin to run with those visions and act on them. The purpose is for you to bless your world with them.

It's wakeup time.

Tool 2: Your Imagination

God created you uniquely for a reason to be able to fulfill all the imaginations and thoughts He deposits in your heart. Your imaginations are so important in the dreaming process.

Imagination is like traveling to a different world.

When you imagine, you can believe all that you can see. This is because your imagination has no barriers of space and time.

In the land of imagination, a clerk can see himself as a CEO, a janitor can see himself as a pilot and a cleaner as a principal. Anything is possible with imagination. The truth is, that if you can imagine it, you can achieve it if you work towards it.

When God works with your imagination, you will be able to achieve the unachievable, imagine the unimaginable and believe the unbelievable.

Dreaming is a process whereby you permit yourself to think "outside the box," and your imagination is the bridge that gets you there.

"Dreams are extremely important. You can't 'do' unless you imagine it."
George Lucas

Tool 3: Your Notebook/Writing Pad

Your visions as they are received from God must be written down clearly to be able to run with them effectively.

What you see determines what you become. When what you see is constantly before you, it inspires you to work towards it.

Habakkuk 2:1-3 states
"I will stand like a guard to watch
And place myself at the tower.
I will want to see what to see what he will say to me.
I will wait to learn how God will answer my complaint.
The Lord answered me. Write down the vision,
Write it clearly on clay tablets
So, whoever reads it, can run to tell others.
It is not yet time for the message to come true.
But that time is coming soon;
It may seem like a long time,
But be patient and wait for it,
Because it will surely come,
It will not be delayed."

As you can see in the Scripture, God gave some instructions which can be applied to our lives. Anytime we go to the Master we can receive instructions on how to run our life or decisions to make regarding certain areas of our life. When we go to God in prayer for help, He expects us to write down the answers He gives us and run with them.

Whatever He tells you is not to be wasted.

What does writing it down do for you?

- Writing your visions and dreams ensures you don't forget them.
- Writing your visions challenges you to do them because it speaks to you.

- Writing your visions helps you to take them back to God when it seems like things are not working because they is constantly before you.

Tool 4: Your Dream Board

Dream boards and books have really impacted my life. I learned about them from Terri Savelle Foy a few years ago and they have changed my life.

A dream board is simply a cork board which you could buy from any store.

Your dream board should show things that are important to you. It should show the things you are passionate about.

In our house, for example, I encourage every member of my family to have a dream board.

We also have the family dream board to show what we are trusting God with our dreams and goals.

My daughter Divine is seven years old but she told us when she was about four and a half that she wanted to be a doctor when she grew up, so she could care for other people and help make them better.

At every opportunity, she continually emphasizes this goal. When we were making a dream board this year, she wanted me to cut out a picture of a doctor to represent her.

She also likes gymnastics and wants to pursue that sport. She asked for a picture of "Simone Biles," an Olympic medalist to be added to her dream board.

She said Simone would help her to aspire to be that good.

My first son, Fikayomi has been a soccer boy ever since he was little and everyone who knows him knows that. He wants to play professional soccer, so as we encourage him; he learned that whatever he was passionate about, he had to add to his dream board. If you meet him today, you will know all about him by just looking at his dream board.

"What you see is what you become."
Author unknown

"As a man thinketh in his heart so is he."
Proverbs 23:7

"The more you think about it, the more you see it, the more you see it, the more you will be stirred up to do it."
Olu Olabode

Like I said, your dream board is simple to make. First, you get a cork board or a simple poster board from the store. Then, gather photos or magazine cut-outs that represent each of your goals. Adding pictures really makes it come alive. I also like to add quotes and scriptures to my dream board. This inspires me and reminds me of my dreams as I look at it daily.

Adding pictures makes it come alive. I also like to add quotes that would inspire me when I look at the board.

However, you can make it plain or fancy. It's your choice. Remember being creative is up to you.

I have included a few samples of what dreams boards could look like on the next couple of pages.

Sometimes I get so inspired that I make dream boards for other people as gifts. It's a thoughtful way to invest in those you care about, and it's inexpensive too!

Dream boards are so powerful because they act as fuel for your vision. The key thing about a dream board is not just making it, but putting it in a strategic place where you can see it every day. I find seeing it challenges you every time you walk past it.

We know that when you put pictures where you can see them, they stir you up. I know that for me, anytime I see my dream board, I am drawn to speak a word and pray over it. I find speaking over it helps me to believe it will happen, and that process will grow even more dreams in my heart.

In our house, we normally pray over each other's dream board once a month to strengthen our belief in God and to cover those dreams in prayers.

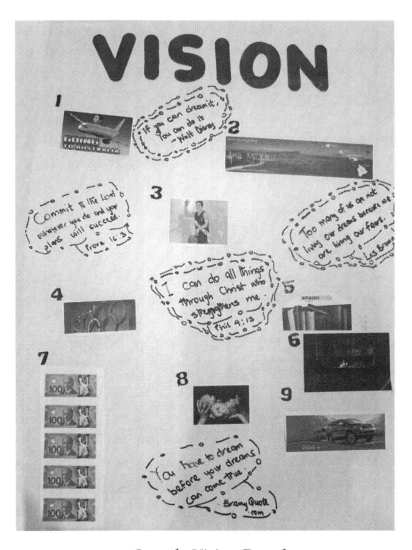

Sample Vision Board

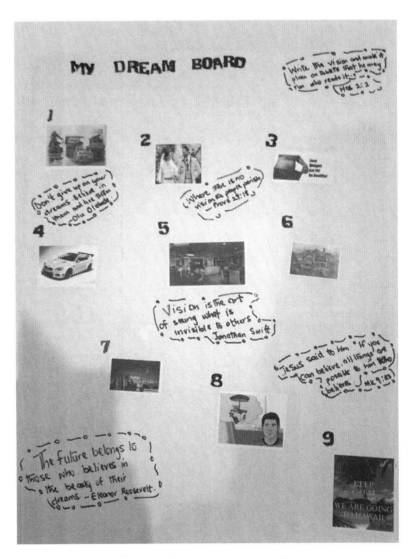

Sample Dream Board

Tool 5: Your Dream Book

A companion to your dream board would be your dream book. A dream book is a notebook with your dreams, goals, and visions written in it. A dream book can also be used as a journal. You write your dreams and the dates which you received them.

Your dream book is where you keep your dreams covered up. It's like your written prayer chamber.

For me, whenever God gives me a new dream or vision, whenever He whispers something new for me to do, I write it down in my dream book, so I can refer to it and constantly pray over those dreams.

Some of those dreams have not yet happened. However, there are others which have already happened. How do I know the difference? Because I wrote them down. I try to go through my dream book once a week, so I can encourage myself with the promises God has given. I found the more I look through my dream book, the more I believe with God's help, I can achieve every dream in my heart.

Ephesians 3:20
"Now to Him Who (by in consequence of) the (action of his) power that is at work within us is able to (carry out His purpose and) do superabundantly, far over and above all that we (dare) ask or think {infinitely beyond our highest prayers, desires, thoughts, hopes or dreams}"

For example, I was looking through my dream book about a month ago, and noticed that about three years ago, I had written a confession trusting God that my books would be sold at the House of James, a bookstore in Abbotsford, BC, on Amazon.com and Barnes and Noble Bookstore.

At the time, I did not know how this was going to be possible as I had not even written any books but I had been praying for help and confessing that it would happen.

Now two years later, some of it has happened and I know that the book being sold in Barnes and Noble is only a matter of time

Is this a coincidence?

I don't think so.

What is it that you can dream? I would encourage you to write it down.

"Whatever You can dream, you can believe
Whatever You can believe, you can achieve"
Olu Olabode

Tool 6: Your Listening & Obedient Heart

Over and over, we see individuals in the Bible miss the blessings of God because of disobedience. Obedience is simply adhering to instructions given. When God gives instructions, you are expected to receive them thankfully and follow them as commanded.

You are not expected to argue with, struggle with or disdain such instructions, because the One directing you knows all things and expects you to trust Him to lead you along the right path.

Let's look at the story of Lot's wife in **Genesis 19:17**. The angels told Lot and his wife and daughters, to escape to the mountains so they would not be destroyed. As they fled from Sodom, they were told not to look back. Did Lot's wife listen? No! She had too much at stake. She could not part with her lifestyle and her "stuff." She loved them so much that she had to disobey instructions. As a consequence of her disobedience, she turned into a pillar of salt. (vs.26)

Another person we can learn from is King Saul. The prophet Samuel instructed Saul to destroy the Amalekites in **1st Samuel 15:1-26**. God told Saul to destroy all the men, women children and animals. Saul killed all the people. However, he kept some of the animals. When confronted by the prophet Samuel, Saul tried to excuse his behavior by blaming it on his people. They took the animals to offer them as a sacrifice to God.

Samuel said that as a result of this disobedience, God would take the kingdom away from Saul and his family.

Saul and David each had a different heart toward God.

David was a man that had an obedient, tender heart towards God and was always willing to repent when he did wrong. He loved God with all his heart and would always put Him first regardless of what the people said or did.

Saul, on the other hand, was the opposite. He was always so bothered about "What the people would say" that he did not have time to cultivate his love or relationship with God.

One of the tools that will aid you in bringing your dreams to pass effectively, is to have a listening and obedient heart. God will test your heart from time to time to see if you will obey Him in the little things before He gives you the bigger assignments.

Abraham was tested when God asked him to take his only son to the mountain to sacrifice him. Abraham passed the test.

David was tested when he was anointed, but not immediately given the kingdom to rule. He passed all the tests he was given.

Lot's wife was tested when she was asked to leave Sodom and Gomorrah and not look back. She did not pass the test but instead turned into a pillar of salt.

Saul was tested when he was instructed to kill the Amalekites and destroy all their possessions. He did not pass the test.

As God puts dreams in your heart. He will want to make sure that your heart is turned towards Him and not "things." Hence, you may go through many tests.

Are you going to pass the tests or will you be found to be a failure? You alone can decide.

"If you are willing and obedient, you will eat the good things of the land."
Isaiah 1:19 (NIV)

"If you will only obey me, you will have plenty to eat."
Isaiah 1:19 (NLT)

In the achievement of your dreams, if you want to eat the good of the land, seek to obey God in every little detail.

I remember while listening to Frank Edwards (a Nigerian gospel artist) give his testimony. When he was informed that he had made his first million naira from selling his CD's, he called his mum to tell her. He said she straight away reminded him that the money did not belong to him but to God since it was the first profit made and was to be "his first fruit" offering unto God.

He said it was hard giving away the money, but God told him that if he gave the first away, He (God) would surprise Frank and take him higher.

Frank said that; looking back, he can say that God has surpassed what He promised him. Obedience and a listening heart is key to receiving whatever God has planned for you.

When you listen, as you meditate, you are required

to obey all the instructions God gives you. Obedience is what opens doors that you cannot comprehend.

My Testimony

As I meditated and asked God questions about my life, I received instructions that took my writing to where it is today.

I remember asking God what He wanted me to do in my current season of life. He then reminded me that I used to write as a little girl. As I pondered on this, He asked me to go out and buy a pack of 3 x 5 index cards and start journaling whatever He spoke to me in my quiet time with Him.

That same day, I went out to buy the cards. I started journaling the next day. He asked me to write on one index card each day. He asked to write whatever he spoke to me about in my devotional time with him. (Writing on the index cards indicated choosing a verse for each of the cards and writing about each of the verses as inspired by God)

I remember saying "Lord I struggled with one card, how am I going to write on three cards? Guess what, as I trusted him, He always gave me the Scriptures, the messages and the prayer points to use.

I did not know that God was increasing my capacity to write. All I did was follow those instructions as He gave them.

After a couple of months, He increased the writing to five index cards per day. That seemed so impossible, but as I trusted Him again, He helped me. Some days while I was listening to the radio, God would give me the Scriptures I would use for that day.

Sometimes, while I was in a conversation, God would speak through the person with whom I was conversing. He truly was my help.

He eventually told me after a couple of months that the index cards I was writing were to become a devotional called "*Throne Time*."

At that time, there were only two months until the end of the year, so God asked me to count how many index cards I would have to write each day to have a complete devotional with 366 days of the year.

I calculated and found out I had to write eight devotionals every day. It was a hard task but I knew God was going to help me.

31st December, 2015 was the date He gave me as the deadline to finish writing the manuscript. When I completed the task, it was such an exciting day. I could not believe that I had completed it

NOTES

CHAPTER 3

THE 5 D'S OF A DREAM

A dream must be conceived, birthed, and nurtured for it to come into manifestation.

Birthing a dream may seem easy, but between conception and birthing, all hell may break loose. When I conceived my third child, I was excited new life was growing in me. However, it was not a smooth pregnancy. When I was four and a half months pregnant, I went for my first scan and was told that my baby had Hydrocephalus which is commonly known as "Water on the brain."

I rejected the doctor's report, but had to constantly trust God that the baby would be born healthy. I had to have eight scans done for this pregnancy with various specialists. When it was time to give birth, my son was born with no negative medical conditions. He is the biggest and strongest of my children. He is the one who eats the most and never falls sick.

I, however, had to go through the pregnancy process and not believe what I was told, so that a healthy, happy baby could be born.

In the same way, a dream must also go through a process, and it involves five stages which we will look at in detail.

1. Download the dream

Downloading entails receiving a thing from its source. It means there is no interception between you and the source when the process of downloading is going on. Downloading for a believer happens when you are waiting on God.

Downloading the dream is the place of receiving the dream from the dream-giver. (God) When you get an email with an attachment, it remains as an attachment which can't be read until it is downloaded.

Downloading the dream is when the dream is received into your spirit. It is when your mind begins to understand the dream. That is when you begin to digest what you have received.

2. Develop the dream

Development is the time of preparation and the time when the dream is being prepared to manifest.

Developing the dream involves nurturing.

What does it take to nurture a child you may wonder?

I would say it takes many steps. The same way it takes commitment to nurturing a child, it also takes commitment to nurture a dream. One thing a lot of people do not know is that nurturing a baby starts when it is conceived in the womb.

Before a woman gives birth; there is a preparation time, there is a time of about nine months between the conception and delivery. These nine months are key to the life of that child.

Nurturing is the process of caring for and encouraging the growth or development of someone or something.

Developing the dream entails asking questions about how the dream will be carried out. It involves finding out what strategies you need to put in place.

I would say in downloading your dream, "thinking time" is highly recommended. This is when you take time away from the busyness of life to meditate upon those dreams.

In "thinking time," you can process information better because you are quiet. You are also able to mull it over and over in your mind until you get a better understanding. God speaks to you in ways you would not normally hear when you are busy. Now, you can muse over your dreams. "Musing" is the act of reflecting on a matter. It can be compared to "chewing the cud." Animals which chew the cud are those that digest their food and then regurgitate it from their first stomach. (Most have four stomachs)

In simple terms, they eat it and bring it back up again.

3. Decide to be obedient

In the process of living your dreams, following instructions is so very important. Instructions enable you to know what to do.

When you download the dream, you begin to understand what it entails. It leads you to the task of developing the dream. As you prepare and ask questions, God will begin to give you instructions. He will not, however, give you a new instruction until you have obeyed and completed the last one. This tells you that you need to be obedient if you want Him to give you further instructions.

Instructions were the big "thing" that kick-started my writing career. As I shared in an earlier chapter, it was in the place of asking questions in my thinking time that I received instructions to go and buy a pack of 3 x 5 index cards. As I followed that instruction, others came one after the other.

Are there instructions that you have received in your thinking time? What have you done with them?

"God will not give you a new instruction past your last level of obedience"
Mike Murdock

I would love to challenge you to listen as you pray. Meditate, and as you receive instructions, make up your mind to follow them. I have found that my level of obedience to instructions will determine if I will receive further instructions or not.

I learnt a very important lesson on Obedience.

Obedience is key to God revealing and leading me into His best for me.

I can tell you that writing on those eight index cards every day was not all fun. Some days I was tired, other days I did not feel like writing, but I had to be diligent and disciplined while keeping the goal of finishing as the focus to motivate me.

Writing this devotional helped me enlarge my capacity to write. It also stirred me up to write more books such as *"Discover, Develop and Deploy Your Gifts"* which became my first published book in January, 2017 and this book which you are now reading.

While writing "*Discover, Develop and Deploy Your Gifts,*" I did not know how I was going to publish the book but I just knew I wanted to write and I just wrote. I did not know how God was going to bring it to pass, but I was obedient to write.

One day in February 2016, I had gone to my husband's office to complete some tasks. On getting there, I met a couple and another lady. They had come to ask if they could use our building for an author's fair.

I walked in on their conversation. My husband, David, introduced me and mentioned that I was writing a book. They showed their excitement and asked if I would like to be part of the author's fair as a writer who was in the writing process. I was so excited that I agreed to do that.

We had the author's fair and it was very successful.

The most exciting part of it was that I got to meet other authors and that further fueled my love for writing and encouraged me to believe I could also be an author.

I did not know then, that when God asked me to start writing on those index cards, He had begun to plan the opportunities and line up the people that were going to help me achieve those dreams He had put in my heart.

When I met that couple in my husband's office, I did not know that they were established publishers. I was just diligent at my writing not worried about the details of publishing the book.

To cut a long story short, that same couple were the ones who helped me with the book proofs, the editing, and a guide to help me in sections in the book where I made mistakes. They not only did that, but they also believed in me and sowed into my life in ways that I could not fathom. They got me a sponsor who paid for the first twenty-four copies of my book even before I had finished writing the book. They published my book at no cost to me. To my surprise, they even marketed my book on Amazon!

I could not fathom the favor of God upon my life and how God could bless me with such blessings.

You might wonder, why I am sharing my story with you? It is to encourage you that when God gives you a dream, He can bring it to pass.

During the time that I was writing that first book, there were days that life seemed so stormy. Challenges came at me from left, right and centre, but I chose to rejoice and trust God to bring an end to every storm.

Joseph was a man in the Bible who encountered storms. He was thrown into a pit, he went to prison, he was lied against, he was forgotten but guess what! He triumphed through it all because God was with him. When God is with you, no matter what challenges come against you, you will triumph.

4. Determine to face all challenges – Never give up!

Challenges! Challenges! Challenges!
I found some interesting quotes about challenges that I would like to share with you.

1. "Challenges are what make life interesting. Overcoming them is what makes them meaningful."
   Pintrest.com

2. "When life puts you in tough situations, don't say" Why me, just say, Try me."
   InspirationBoost.com

3. Challenges make you discover things about yourself that you never really knew. "They're what make the instrument stretch, what makes you go beyond the norm."
   Active Titan

4. "We don't use our faith to get rid of problems, we use it to remain calm during problems." **John Hagee.**

5. "God promises to make something good out of the storms that bring devastations to your life." **Romans 8:28**

6. "No matter how many times you fall, always stay strong and have the courage. Get back up again. Never give up! " **Jarofquotes.com**

7. "Life is full of setbacks and rejection. You will fail at times and at times, you will be scared too. Don't ever give up and eventually you will succeed beyond your wildest dreams." **quoteswarehouse.com**

8. "If you want to reach a goal, you must see the reaching in your own mind before you actually arrive at your goal." **quoteswave.com**

9. "We don't grow when things are easy; We grow when we face challenges." **PicsLordsPlan.com**

The last quote I just shared says it all.
Challenges are what cause us to grow.

You would notice that when you don't have any problems, when there is nothing keeping you on your toes, you would just take life as it comes. However, when challenges hit you, what happens? You begin to look for a way out! You don't mind whatever it takes to get you out of that situation. You just want to be out.

The Bible states in *James 1;2-4 (NIV)*

"Count it all joy, my brothers when you meet trials of various kinds, for you know that the testing of your faith produces steadfastness. And let steadfastness have its full effect that you may be perfect and complete, lacking in nothing."

This tells me every human being will go through challenges. However, one must not let those challenges discourage us permanently.

I must rise when I fall. You must rise when you fall. When I am going through a challenge, I always remember the words of my late dad. While growing up, my dad had only one phrase for whatever we were going through.

That phrase was "Everything in life is for a little while."

That phrase has really helped me over the years to see that problems are only temporary. They are subject to change. Hence, whatever obstacles we face in living our dreams, we must choose to turn them into stepping stones. Do not let them dominate us; rather we need to choose to conquer and overcome them.

I have faced so many challenges in my life. I mentioned earlier, that in 2006, my husband and I were told by doctors that the baby I was carrying had "water on his brain." I refused the report of the doctor and we kept praying. When that baby was born, there was no sign of any "water on the brain," He is my healthiest child, the strongest, the smartest and never falls sick.

In 2011, at eight years of age, my oldest son was diagnosed with Leukemia. We went through three and a half years of treatment.

He also had a heart infection during this time and we almost lost him, but I thank God that today he is free of all medications and is completely healed. He has become a living testimony.

In years past, my husband and I had numerous dreams about our second son being injured in various ways. We had to keep praying for him for years so that the things we saw would not take place. I've had financial challenges in life. I have had educational challenges while in middle school and have had various setbacks and could go on and on.

Why am I giving all these examples?

These challenges caused me to grow. I learned how to overcome them through prayer, standing on the Word of God, persevering, and refusing to give up.

It's your turn to persevere. Even while writing this book, I have had some challenges. One was that after writing the first two chapters of the book, I just had a mental block. For about one month, I could not write.

I just could not move past those first two chapters.

Every time I sat down, nothing happened. No direction, no inspiration, no revelation. It was frustrating, but one day I sat down as usual and said, "Holy Spirit, I am way past the deadline I set to finish this book. You have to help me; I cannot do it myself."

It was as if a dam was opened; I began to write and write and write. He began to speak to me and show me what to do. It was as if I had never stopped.

What am I trying to say? Don't give up. Keep persevering. Your dreams will become a reality.

5. Demonstrate the attitude of a winner
Be joyful in all situations

James 1:2 states that we should count it all joy when we face trials, troubles, disappointments, struggles of life, stormy seas of life" (paraphrased)

Is that going to be easy to do?

No, I assure you that it's not. One thing I know however is in having an attitude of joy because that is where our strength comes from.

You must be intentional about joy. You must be able to see past the problem at hand. You must allow yourself to visualize the problem being solved.

It's like an athlete, Before he/she runs the race, he/she must have pictured him/herself winning that race. It is a matter of perspective. A winner is a person who sees the impossible becoming possible, regardless of the obstacles on the journey.

What is joy?

Joy is an emotion that comes out of our spirit man. Joy is not happiness. Happiness reflects the happy events that happen in our lives - money in our account, when we are healthy, when everything is going well and favourable in our lives.

Joy, however, cannot be explained. It does not depend on how favourable an event is to you. It flows from within your spirit. It relies on knowing the kind of God you serve. It rests on the ability of what God can do and not what is happening in the environment around a person.

Joy, I find. is infectious. When we are joyful, people around us cannot stay miserable for a long time. It has a form of enthusiasm and peace that comes along with it. Joy cannot really be explained but it connotes great delight. What I love most about it is that when there is no money in the bank, no food in the house and no idea of how things would be sorted out, a person with an attitude of joy will always overcome.

This is because when we embrace joy, it gives us the strength to fight the battle. It gives us the strength to move forward in the storms even when we cannot see where we are going.

We can see this in the life of King David in the Bible. When he was a child, he had to go through various challenges. His father did not really value him and his brothers did not like him. While growing up, other people were envious of him. Saul sought to kill him because the people sang about him. He had to go through various challenges. He had to wait for thirteen years after he had been anointed before becoming the king.

David, however, had a peaceful demeanor through it all. He never grumbled against any of these people neither did he fight them. Rather, he got closer to God thereby getting the strength to go through his challenges until the time that he became king.

He demonstrated the attitude of a winner. (*1ˢᵗ Samuel 16:11-13, 2ⁿᵈ Samuel 22: 4*)

Psalm 19:8 states

"The commandments of the Lord are right, bringing joy to the heart.

The commands of the Lord are clear, giving insight for living."

Do you need some joy in your life? Do things seem like they are not working out as they should? David said he got his joy from the word of God. That's your clue!

Do you need strength for the journey?

Do you need some joy in your life to thrust you forward?

Do you want to demonstrate the attitude of a winner?

Ask the joy-giver today, and He will fill you to overflowing.

When you are joyful, nothing can stop those dreams from manifesting because even if you encounter difficulties, you know they are only stepping stones.

"The joy of the Lord is your strength."
Nehemiah 8:10

CHAPTER 4

BREAK OUT OF EVERY NEGATIVE MOLD

It's time to break out of every negative mold around your life. Every successful person had to choose to break out of every wrong mold that had sought to keep them limited.

What is a mold?

A mold is a hollow container used to give shape to molten or hot liquid material (such as wax or metal).

A mold is also described as a distinctive and typical style, form, or character.

A mold is anything that you pattern yourself after. It could be worldly in nature or godly in nature. You are the only one that can decide what mold to be shaped after.

When you look at your character and your style of living (regarding areas of your life such as your finances, health, emotions, physical self, spiritual life and otherwise), what or who do you pattern it after.

Molds can be negative or positive in nature. A mold could also be a certain way of thinking or doing things.

Romans 12:2 (**Phillips**) states
"Don't let the world around you squeeze you into its mold, but let God re-mold your minds from within, so that you may prove in practice that the plan of God for you is good, meets all his demands and moves towards the goal of true maturity."

The world would always seek to squeeze you into its mold (its culture and its way of doing things). The world frequently frowns upon people who do things differently.

Successful people are successful because they choose to break out of the mold of "average."

Milton Wright was the father of aviation pioneers, Wilbur and Orville Wright. Before they invented and built their plane, their dad had gone to a scientific convention where he was told that metal could not fly.

Six years later, however, his sons launched the first flying machine, breaking out of the "can't do it" mold.

A mold often anchors on a mental idea It is a function of what we think of ourselves and a function of what we believe can happen.

Thomas Edison, who invented the lightbulb failed more than ten thousand times. However, he refused to give up or give into failure. Because of his persistence, he persevered and invented the incandescent light bulb.

Types of Negative Molds
1. Your Excuses
2. Your Self
3. Procrastination
4. Laziness
5. Slothfulness
6. Fear

Please feel free to add to this list. You would know what mold seeks to limit you.

Remolding/Positive/Godly molding is essential for a person to change their way of thinking or mindset.

Proverbs 23:7a states
"For as he thinks in his heart, so is he"

Before a person gives his heart to Jesus, his way of thinking, his character and style of doing things is patterned after the world. You believe you must toil for everything you would have in your life; you believe you must make a way for yourselves.

However, when you give your heart to Jesus, He calls you into a new way of thinking. He calls you into a new kingdom and in this new kingdom, He wants you to change the way you think. He wants you to remold your thinking. He wants you to believe everything you read in the Bible.

Joshua understood that Moses was a very great leader. He, however, could not see himself excelling above his leader until God re-molded him.

God had to continually remind him to be strong and very courageous. He had to get him to focus on the book of the law, to forget all that he knew. He also had to continually encourage Joshua to see himself as strong.

The first way to break out of every negative mold is to change your way of thinking. You must fashion your thinking in line with what God thinks of you.

For years, I had certain mindsets in various areas of my life. Financially I believed that if you did not study certain courses, you could not make certain incomes.

I believed the government had the power to limit your advancement because of the policies they put in place.

I had other areas where I had imposed a negative mold on myself when I think about it. I wonder how I could have let other people dictate the direction of my life.

In the book of Numbers, Moses sent twelve people out to spy on the land of Canaan to see if it was good enough for Israel to enter.

Ten of the spies let what they thought about themselves and what they saw limit them. Nobody called them "grasshoppers," but they came back with the report that "we became like grasshoppers in our own sight, and so we were in their sight." **Numbers 13:33** and because they had the wrong perspective, God stopped them from entering the promised land.

It's a matter of perspective. Your perspective is your way of seeing and viewing things. What are you letting dictate your perspective about life?

With what lens are you looking at life? Are you looking through the lens of God and His Word - *Ephesians 3:20?*

Are you able to do everything you set your mind on? (*Philippians.4:13*) or are you looking through the lens of man, of your friends, your family members, your colleagues at work or the events that happen around you?

You alone decide what lens to use for your life.

Joshua had to choose to be strong and very courageous. He had to let the past remain the past; he also had to stop looking through the lens of Moses. It was the beginning of a new day for him.

For you, it is a new day too.

STOP looking through the lens of the past.
STOP looking through the lens of friends.
STOP looking through the wrong lens.

Break out of every negative mold.
Let God remold your mind.
It's time to renew your mind to the word of God.

Regarding your finances, **renew your mind.**
Regarding your personal life, **renew your mind.**
Regarding your marriage, **renew your mind.**
Regarding your career, **renew your mind.**
Regarding any area of your life, **renew your mind.**

"When you change your thinking, you change your mindset. When you change your mindset, you change your life."
Olu Olabode

People we see who have excelled have had to not let the world squeeze them into its mold.

A lot of times we hear people make statements such as:

"That's not how my parents did it."

"That's not how my teacher taught me."

"You can't do it that way. It's not done."

"That's not how we do it in my family."

Today I would encourage you to begin to search your mind and reflect on how you do things and check what influences you to do things that way.

Is it in line with the way God thinks or otherwise?

Trust me, I have found out that the way we think dictates the way we live as stated in Proverbs 4:23. Our mind is a compass that drives our life. Don't get to the end of your life and find out you lived your life wrong the entire time.

Examples of Negative Mold Breakers

1. Debbie Macomber

Debbie Macomber is a New York bestselling author with over 170,000 million copies of her romance novels in print worldwide. Her books have been brought to life as a television series and made for TV films.

However, her life was not always a fairy tale. Debbie was born and raised in a small town. She always dreamed of being a writer but she did not learn to read until she was 10 and had dyslexia.

Growing up with challenges was hard as she was always at the bottom of her class. Her third-grade teacher told her mum "Debbie is a nice little girl, but she's never going to do well in school" and she didn't. She barely graduated from high school and married as a teenager but always had that dream of being a writer. She, however, did not write for a long time, because she was fearful that people would laugh at her.

How did She overcome Fear?

She was close to a cousin who died of leukemia and Debbie said it was as if God was telling her "You cannot stuff your dreams into the future, if you are going to be a writer, you must start now." She had a list of excuses because of her negative background.

When she started writing, she was a stay at home mum with four small children. She rented a typewriter and used it to write when her children went to bed at night. She got rejected five years in a row by publishers but she did not give up.

One thing I like about Debbie is that even though she works in the secular realm, she brings her faith into her work. She says "You cannot separate Debbie the author from Debbie the Christian, because she loves the Lord. She does not preach but she shows God's love and offers hope in her stories."

The gift God gave her was that of a storyteller but she had to learn to be a writer and that was one of her challenges. She had to write four books. That was her apprenticeship, but she was not going to give up because she really wanted this dream to manifest.

Whenever she wrote, she always used to ask God to guide her words and help her to write her story. She prays about all her story arcs and plots.

2. *Walter Elias Disney*

Walter Elias Disney, who is also known as Walt Disney, truly was a mold breaker. He was a man who believed in his dreams, and as a result, he saw them come to pass. He once said, "**All our dreams can come true if we have the courage to pursue them.**"

Lilian, Walt Disney's wife, played a great role in his life. She was the one who advised him to name his famous mouse Mickey, instead of his preferred name, Mortimer. Listening to his wife ended up being one of the smartest decisions of his life!

Sometimes it takes breaking out of our own molds or ways of doing things, and being open to adapting to change, in order to see our dreams come to pass. Walt Disney was willing to do this by listening to his wife's advice, and boy did it ever pay off!

Today, Mickey Mouse is a universally recognized cultural icon. Disney's numerous films celebrating the triumph of the little guy and the simple charms of small-town life, captured the imaginations of many, fueling the dreams of six generations.

Overcoming Adversity

Walt Disney loved bringing his drawings to life through the magic of animation. Advertising was less than fulfilling however, so he converted his garage into a studio, and with borrowed equipment, he began producing his own shorts, called Laugh-O-Grams.

It wasn't until he teamed up with his shrewd and kindly older brother Roy, who took care of business for him, that Walt began to prosper modestly.

Even so, his first commercially successful creation, Oswald the Lucky Rabbit, was stolen from him. Disney had carelessly allowed the character to be copyrighted, not under his name, but under his distributor's name.

It was a mistake Disney would not repeat.

Searching for a replacement for Oswald, Disney hit upon the idea of creating a new cartoon character based on a mouse that had lived in his office in Kansas City. As Disney liked to tell it, "Mice gathered in my wastebasket when I worked late at night. One of them was my particular friend."

With the help of Roy and Ub Iwerks, an illustrator from his Film Ad days, Disney fleshed out his new character—and Mickey Mouse was born.

As you can see, it takes a tremendous amount of courage to break the mold and see your dreams come to pass. Disney's willingness to dare to dream, accept help from others, and adapt to change, resulted in his dreams becoming a reality! There may be times of opposition, like Walt Disney experienced, but if you are committed to your dreams, you can achieve anything!

Famous Quotes:

Walt had some famous quotes that enabled him to break out of the "normal mold," and helped him become such a success.

"First - Think, Second - Believe, Third - Dream, and finally, Dare"

"All our dreams can come true if we have the courage to pursue them."

"If you can dream it, you can do it!"

"When you are curious, you find lots of interesting things to do."

"It's kind of fun to do the impossible."

"Get a good idea and stay with it. Dog it, and work it until it's done right."

NOTES

CHAPTER 5

ENABLERS OF YOUR DREAMS

1. Your God: your dream giver
2. Your passion
3. Your talents/gifts/abilities
4. Your helpers of destiny.
5. Your confessions

1. *Your God*

You might be wondering why I called Him "Your God" and not just "God." The reason is that if something is yours, you can lay claim to it. You must come to a point where you see God as your only source and your help.

***Psalm 121:1 (AMP)* states**
"I will lift up my eyes to the hills (around Jerusalem, to sacred Mount Zion and Mount Moriah) from whence shall my help come? My help comes from the Lord, who made heaven and earth."

For your dreams to be accomplished, it is necessary to involve Him in the dream process as He is the dream giver. I have found out that when I trust God and ask Him to help me with the dreams He has given. He is able to give me appropriate help for each dream.

Ephesians 3:20 states
"Now to him who is able to do exceedingly abundantly above all that we ask or think according to the power that works in us."

He can help you go and do beyond what you can even comprehend. See God as your helper so that He can act as one. When you hand your dreams over to Him, He takes you beyond all you can even think, dream, imagine or fathom.

2. Your Passion

You may wonder what it means to have a passion for a thing.

The word **"passion"** according to the English Oxford Living Dictionaries (online edition) is "An intense desire or enthusiasm for something" meaning that a person can have a passion for a thing that is important to them.

Passion is an emotion that is very strong and must be directed appropriately. Your passion can lead you to your destiny however it can also lead you to destruction if not properly harnessed.

Passion can be compared to a horse and how submitted it is to human beings. A horse has the natural strength to overpower a human being but it readily submits because it is trained to be submissive to its master. The training is what makes the horse become what you would call "strength under control."

The strength is there but not used except when the horse senses danger and refuses to move towards the point of danger.

Passion is an emotion God put in each one of us to change our world. Passionate people are world changers.

The energy behind all great art, all great music, all great literature, the driving force behind all great drama and all great architecture is passion.

Passion makes all things great.

The Webster's 1828 Dictionary defines "passion" as "a zeal, vehement desire, a love for something."

Passion mobilizes armies to sacrifice of themselves in battle. Nothing great is done or achieved without passion.

Passion is the driving force behind scientific inventions. Passion turns the impossible to possible. Without passion, life becomes boring and dull.

Isaiah 37:32, Psalm 69:9

God wants you and I to live a passionate life. He wants you and me to sense the passion that he has put within reach of us and utilize it. *Mark 2:1-5*

Are you passionate about Living?

You need to ask yourself the question "Am I passionate about living?" If your answer is No, then you may need to dig deep within yourself to find out why.

The Apostle Paul says in *Colossians 3:2*

"Whatever you do, do it with all your heart as unto the Lord and unto not as unto men."

He says no matter what you do, do it passionately.

God wants you to be intentional and use your God-given sense of passion. *Romans 12:11*

3. *Your talents, gifts, abilities*

You have a gift! I have a gift! The woman on the street, the man in prison has a gift. We all have gifts that were given us when we were born. However, as much as it is good to know you have a gift, it is much more important to find out how that gift can be developed and used in your life and in your world.

You might be wondering what do I mean by a "gift?" A gift here refers to natural ability, talent, or skill (flair, aptitude, facility, bent, ability, capacity, and expertise).

A gift refers to the ability or potential you were endowed with when you were created. No one was born empty; everyone was born with a gift or multiple gifts. This gift could also refer to the skills you have been able to develop while you have been on this earth.

These gifts have a wide range. They could be creative such as dance, drama, choreography, creative arts, modeling, building, drawing, designing, sewing. They could be skills developed in a trade such as automobiles, construction, welding, woodworking, crocheting, knitting, and hairdressing.

You could have an excellent fashion sense. These gifts could be skills such as leadership skills and organizational skills. (Do you have strong attention to detail?)

They could be culinary skills (baking, catering, cooking, event planning). They could be communication skills (writing, teaching, speaking, coaching, training) they could be sales and marketing skills (which you need to effectively run a business).

In this age of information technology, do you have proficient computer skills? (web design, info design, web marketing, media design, an SEO specialty?) do you have skills in TV, film, or video?

Do you love photography, do you have people skills, do you have the gift of mercy, of helps, of listening, of compassion? Are you called to open an orphanage or take prostitutes off the street? I could go on and on.

So have you discovered your gift?

If you have, what are you doing with it?

Culled from ***Discover, Develop and Deploy Your Gift*** — my first book.

4. *Your Helpers of Destiny*

These enablers of a dream are very important in your "dream journey." Whatever it is, God has put upon your heart to do; there are people, He has ordained to help you in this journey.

These helpers of destiny are people God has ordained to assist and help you bring to pass the dreams in your heart. You may wonder, "How will I locate my helpers of destiny?" I have learned that as you step out to run with those dreams, God will direct each of the destiny helpers to you at the right time. I discovered that when you are obedient to follow instructions you have been given, things begin to fall into place as they should.

When my book was published, a friend, I will call her a sister who I have known for a couple of years, saw the book on Facebook and sent me a message asking if I would like to do an audiobook version of the book.

I was shocked. I could almost not believe it because I had thought of having an audio book but did not know how I was going to do it. We are currently working on that project and I am thankful and grateful for bringing this sister into my life.

God has ordained people to help you bring your

dreams to pass. Have you connected with them yet? I would encourage you to trust God with your dreams and pray God will send you your destiny helpers.

Another key I would love to leave with you is that you must be sensitive to the opportunities and people God is sending you, because sometimes those people do not come dressed as you expect.

Culled from my first book *Discover, Develop and Deploy Your Gift*.

5. Your Confessions

According to Bill Winston, an American preacher, author, visionary leader, businessman and entrepreneur, "Your confessions mean to say the same thing God is saying and not what people are saying. Speak his word." He said "God can do all things, if you believe it. If you believe, all things are possible; your part is to speak it and God's part is to do it."

We can see this from a story in the Bible found in *Numbers 13:1-33.* Twelve spies were sent out to spy the land but Joshua and Caleb believed and spoke that they could conquer the land. The ten other spies insisted that they were not able to conquer the land. They said "we became like grasshoppers in our own sight, and so we were in their sight." It was just a perception of themselves.

Guess what? This wrong perception stopped the ten spies and all Israelites above the age of twenty from entering the promised land.

In **Numbers 14:26-34**, God got so tired of their incessant complaints that He decided to give them what they spoke out. How sad! Only Caleb and Joshua were spared because of the fruit of their lips.

Your confessions are the accessories God uses to bring about the accomplishment of your dreams.

> "From the fruit of their mouth a person's stomach is filled; with the harvest of their lips they are satisfied. The tongue has the power of life and death, and those who love it will eat its fruit."
> **Proverbs 18:20-21 (NIV)**

Whatever you want to see in your life, you must "call forth" with your mouth. You must speak them out.

> "It is written "I believe therefore I have spoken," Since we have that same spirit of faith, we also believe and therefore speak."
> **2 Corinthians 4:13**

> "As it is written, "I have made you the father of many nations" in the presence of the God whom he believed, who gives life to the dead and calls into existence the things that do not exist."
> **Romans 4:17 (ESV)**

God wants us to call things, things that do not exist, into existence." You and I are speaking spirits just like Jesus so He is waiting for us to decree into our atmosphere what we want to see.

We are born to dominate and speak whatever we want to see into our environment.

To dominate means "to have a commanding influence on, exercise control over." it also means to rule over, govern, control. The Latin word "*dominus*" meaning "master" gives us the root word "*domin*."Words from the Latin *dominus* have to do with being another's master; hence "to dominate" is to have power and control over, as if being someone's master.

Do not let situations dominate you, rather speak your dreams into existence. If you truly believe in them, the Bible tells you to speak.

Remember you have the power of life and death in your mouth. You have a miracle in your mouth, so don't let negative situations remain unchanged. Start speaking today and turn them around for good.

The words you speak control your destiny. Choose what to speak. Speak life!

We have been talking a great deal about dreams in this book, but the climax of this book should be —What am I going to do with all I have read?

Are you going to just lay the book aside when you are finished reading it or are you going to get up and begin to run with your dreams (if you are not already doing so?)

Yes, it is time to begin to pour yourself into your world.

NOTES

CHAPTER 6

YOUR WORLD IS WAITING

"For the earnest expectation of the creatures waiteth for the manifestation of the sons of God."
Romans 8:19 (KJV)
"The created world itself can hardly wait for what's coming next. Everything in creation is being held back."
Romans 8:19 (MSG)

Are you holding back everything in your sphere of influence or the people that have been ordained to be affected by you?

Are you fulfilling your assignment in life?

Are you fulfilling a purpose or just passing time?

Remember time does not wait for anyone. It keeps moving and you better be moving with it or else one day you'll wake up and realize, "Oh no! I'm 50 years old. What have I done with my time and my life?"

It's time to use whatever you have been given so

that you don't lose it. The dreams you have been given are for a reason. Don't let them go to waste.

Do you know that when you are faithful in little things, you will be given more? The question is, are you faithful in little things, are you faithful to follow instructions you have been given?

God is waiting to reward your faithfulness. Remember He put those dreams in your heart and He will ask you at the end of your life what you have done with His dreams.

Living your dream tips

Seek to impact your generation
Be a blessing to someone
Look at life's obstacles as stepping stones.
Refuse to be moved by what you see
Refuse to be stagnant
Keep moving forward.

APPENDICES

QUOTES ON DREAMS AND GOALS

- "A dream is a goal with a deadline."
  Napoleon Hill

- "Let's plant out dreams in this garden and entwine ourselves like vines."
  Unknown

- "You are never too old to set another goal or to dream a new dream."
  C. S. Lewis

- "All our dreams can come true if we have the courage to pursue them."
  Walt Disney

- "If Howard Schultz gave up after being turned down by banks 242 times; there would be no Starbucks."
  www.pintrest.com

- "If Walt Disney quit too soon, his theme park concept was thrashed 302 times; there would be no Disneyland. "
  www.pintrest.com

- "Believe in your dreams, they were given to you for a reason."
  Katrina Mayer

- "She turned her cants into cans and her cans and her dreams into plans."
  Markayla-bayla.tumbler.com

- "If you can dream it, you can have it."
  Walt Disney

- "Go Confidently in the direction of your dreams, Live the life you've always imagined."
  Unknown

- "When the vision is clear, the result will appear."
  Terri Savelle Foy

- "Goals in writing are dreams with deadlines."
  Unknown

- "The reason we have dreams is so we can follow them. Dare to live."
  Livin3.com

- "Do not give up on your dreams, goals or the gifts God has given you."
BibleGodQuotes.com

- "If you don't imagine, nothing ever happens at all."
John Green

- "The future belongs to those who believe in the beauty of their dreams."
Eleanor Roosevelt

- "Motivation is when your dreams put on work clothes."
Unknown

- "There are those who look at things they were and ask why? I dream of things that never were and ask why not?"
Robert Kennedy

- "We grow by great dreams. All big men are dreamers."
Woodrow Wilson

- "God gives us dreams a size too big so that we can grow in them."
Unknown

- "Vision without action is a daydream. Action without vision is a nightmare."
  Japanese proverb

- "Your aspirations are your possibilities."
  Samuel Johnson

- "If you can dream it, God can do it."
  Terri Savelle Foy

END NOTES

Article (Jesusalive.cc)

Oxford Dictionary.com

Walt Disney, Biography
www.justdisney.com

12 Walt Disney Quotes
www.brightdrops.com

Keynotes, Leadership- The Disney Way
http://www.capojac.com

Walt Disney - Wikipedia ,en.m.wikipedia.org

Author Debbie Macomber Shares Her Triumph Over Dyslexia The Christian Broadcasting Network www.cbn.com>700club>guests>bios

The Everyday Life Bible (Containing the Amplified Old Testament and the New Amplified New Testament, Notes and Commentary by Joyce Meyer) Additional text copyright @2006 by Joyce Meyer.

Holy Bible, New Living Translation, Compact Edition, 1996, 2006 by Tyndale Charitable Trust.

Noah Webster 1828 Online Dictionary

ABOUT THE AUTHOR

You can connect with Olu on the following platforms.

https://www.facebook.com/Olu-Olabode-Impact-Foundation-1759159980789236/
Youtube.com/oluolabode
Twitter.com/oluolabode
Instagram.com/olu.olabode

You can also listen to encouraging, inspirational and faith-building messages on my Youtube channel "dreamsofthehearttv."

Contact Olu for more information on her charity, the Olu Olabode Impact Foundation.

You may contact

Olu Olabode

email: info@oluolabode.com
website: www.oluolabode.com

Olu's first book

Discover, Develop and Deploy Your Gifts
ISBN: 978-1-895112-375

Available from
Amazon.com
http://amzn.to/2tcsRJf

Olu's books are also available on
www.oluolabode.com

To contact the publisher:

HeartBeat Productions Inc.
Box 633
Abbotsford, BC Canada V2T 6Z8
email: info@heartbeat1.com
604.852.3769

Made in the USA
Columbia, SC
15 May 2018